FACEBOOK ADVERTISING 2018

The Ultimate step-by-step guide to Facebook Advertising and Social Media Marketing

(Bonus Beginner lessons: How to generate leads and successful Ad case studies)

By

Dale Anderson and Ultimate Marketing Guides

Copy right © Dale Anderson

All rights reserved. The following is the work of the aforementioned author and no parts of this book may be published, republished or sold without the express consent of the author.

ISBN-13:978-1722095062

ISBN-10:1722095067

CONTENT

INTRODUCTION

BACKGROUND

THE ROLE OF SOCIAL MEDIA IN ADVERTISING

CHAPTER 1: THE WORLD OF FACEBOOK ADVERTISING

Why Facebook?

ABC of Facebook advertising: understanding Facebook ads

Why ads thrive on Facebook

CHAPTER 2: CREATING FACEBOOK ADS

Is Facebook advertising right for your business?

Choosing the right marketing objective

Choosing ad placements, budget and schedule

Ad placements

Setting a campaign budget

Choosing a delivery schedule for your ads

Choosing the optimum budget: the $1 rule versus the golden rule

CHAPTER 3: TARGETING

Defining your audience

Facebook audience insights: doing a demographic research

Creating the ideal ad copy and image

Lead generation and conversion with Facebook ads

CHAPTER 4: CREATING A PROFITABLE FACEBOOK MARKETING CAMPAIGN

Setting a campaign goal

Measuring the impacts of your ads

Leveraging the Facebook pixel

Benefits of using Facebook analytics

CHAPTER 5: CONCLUSIONS

Dos and don'ts of Facebook advertising

Case studies A: successful ads

Case studies B: Dead ads

WRAP UP

INTRODUCTION

In the first quarter of 2012, Facebook bagged a total of $872 million in advertising revenue, a figure that jumped twelve-fold at the end of the first quarter of 2018 to a whopping $11 billion.

As staggering as these figures may seem, they should not be impossible to believe, considering the fact that since the beginning of 2018, the social media giant has hosted around 1.45 billion active users on a daily basis and more than 2 billion unique users monthly. And these numbers keep growing!

While it is tempting to believe the tons of negative feedbacks out in the public about how advertising on Facebook, or any other platform for that matter, is a boondoggle, it is apt to ponder over why, to keep abreast with their customers, over a million small businesses have leveraged on the copiousness of the Facebook world to advertise their contents.

The reason behind the ever-expanding advertisement revenue and indeed environment of Facebook is not far-fetched.

Companies seeking to place ads on Facebook do so for a number of reasons, amongst which are: the relatively cheap cost of running ads, great outreach (more customers can be reached on Facebook than on any other social media platform) and creating and maintaining lasting relationships with their customers whilst engaging them constantly with valuable and interesting content.

Another reason why Facebook is the popular choice for adverts placements is the outstanding flexibility of its ads campaign architecture. Users on placing ads can set their ads budget, schedule when they want their ads to run, choose from a variety of contents to advertise (whether it is text, images or videos), define very specifically who they want their ads to reach and measure how effective their ad placements are *vis-à-vis* investment and use that data to maintain, improve or terminate their ad campaigns.

Since Facebook is merely the line connecting the dots of users' relationships with their families and friends, advertisers are assured that content advertised on Facebook would reach not only the users who can view them directly, but also some others who would come to have knowledge of them through peer-to-peer interactions.

This is a massive plus for advertisers, who can – and should – efficiently leverage on this stupendous traffic that Facebook commands.

Facebook, indeed, is only one of many such media via which ad placers can showcase their content. Other examples include Google's AdWords, the affiliate marketing web-hub, ClickBank, and other platforms which are reasonably beyond the scope of this text.

Due the reasons earlier stated in this book, Facebook enjoys unmatched powers of reach and targeting, perhaps making it the first stop for marketers who wish to broadcast their products and/or services online.

This potential of Facebook especially, and social media in general, to get a message across to as many people as would be possible through the traditional tele-media in a much more fluid and cost-effective way, lies at the core of the might of this new frontier of content advertising.

Furthermore, looking back at the progress social media has made in these relatively few years of existence, who is to say the extent to which it can expand – or if there are limits at all.

According to the Pew Research Center, roughly 68% (two thirds) of American adults admit they are Facebook users, a vast majority of whom are aged between 18 and 24 years. Going by this statistic, it's safe and paramount to state that the future of human social interaction belongs to social media; a future dominated by Facebook.

BACKGROUND

In the last few decades, communication between two – or indeed any number of – people, has taken a drastic turn.

The advent of the Tele-media (telephone, television, radio), debuting with the telephone in the nineteenth century and peaking with the Farnsworth television in the twentieth, created a panacea for spreading a message across to several thousand people in an instant; the introduction of social media has skyrocketed that number to billions.

It is not an overstatement therefore, to state that social media is the new frontier of efficient and speedy human communication and relationship.

While the aforementioned earlier media outlets or systems remain as relevant today as they were decades ago, it is worthy of note that a major advantage the social media has over its older contemporaries lies in its open-endedness.

A TV program host would, for instance, pass a message across to possible onlookers, without him either knowing or getting simultaneous feedback from his viewers. This is not the case on social media platforms, for as its name suggests, messaging on any social media platform is essentially an active interaction between the poster and the receiver.

This feedback mechanism accounts for the 'hook' social media has on its users. It is literally why one cannot possibly get enough of it, and why hundreds of millions of people floor its arenas annually.

As people started to accept and utilize this new communication tool in their large numbers, another form of usefulness and purpose of it swam ashore.

It was realized that whilst maintaining relationships between themselves and their friends online, users could, on occasion, spare a few seconds to look at a commodity he might be interested in.

They could also make their interest known to the owner of such commodity (who is a user themselves), and, as things would be apt to go, offer to purchase the commodity. This gave rise to social media advertising. The rest, they say, is history.

In the last few years leading to 2018, the world of virtual marketing has made a tremendous leap; from placing disparate photos on a web page to organizing an intricate meshwork of ideas, so designed as to reach specific categories of people, in specified locations, at pre-planned times.

Hence, an advertising campaign could be automated – planned to run all on its own, unencumbered. Though accounts have been given by naysayers of the inertness of virtual advertising, there are whelming evidences to prove that this is not the case.

Several of these accounts are given by thousands of advertisers who, comparing sales of unadvertised with those of advertised products, have come to the conclusion that the massive boost they record in sales of advertised products is due, in fact, to advertising.

Many of these advertisers however, have stated that their debut advertising campaigns ranged from not-so-good to absolute disasters, and that perseverance and a constant improvement in planning have been responsible for their eventual success.

It is therefore adequate to conclude that while success in advertising is very often guaranteed, it is not a given; meticulous planning is still needed, and that is what this book aims to offer.

THE ROLE OF SOCIAL MEDIA IN ADVERTISING

The concept of modern day social networking was born in a dorm in the early 2000's, a story we all are familiar with. But what we might not have seemed to grasp is the maddening explosion of the social media particularly in the last decade (about 42% of the world's population is on social media!).

It was gathered that in five years, the number of registered users on three of the biggest social networking platforms, Facebook, Twitter and Instagram, jumped from a little more than 600 million in 2010 to over 2 billion in 2015 – which is the number of active users of Facebook alone in 2018.

In the same span of years, the amount of video content uploaded on YouTube leapt from 24 hours to 300 hours per minute, and the number of web blogs rose from 152 million to 1 billion. And we can go on and on with the numbers.

Social media as it is, is currently the most utilized of mechanisms, with the average person spending a sizeable chunk of their time on it daily,

This fact is in congruence with the results of a research that shows that within the last decade, social media adoption has jumped from less than 10% in 2005 to nearly 70% in 2013. And perhaps, another fact to consider is that about 40% of elderly people are on several social media platforms.

This shows beyond doubt that the adoption of social media is devoid of any age restriction, and that in truth, social media has come to stay.

In the wake of the inevitability of social media to completely dominate human interactions in the nearest future (if it hasn't done so already), it's not only wise to rip off of this global trend a handsome amount of utility, but also shockingly easy, quick and cheap to do so.

The financial implications, and indeed the ease, of posting content on say Facebook, are inexistent, lined astride the costs of running same on local television or radio; little wonder the American business tycoon (and president, as at the time of this writing) has taken a prudent step towards leveraging on the advantages inherent in the use of social media to carry out such activities as posting news and dictating policies, as a way of reaching out directly to the people.

Multinational companies, industries, sport clubs, restaurants, coffee shops, and small cafés alike are not left out of the trend, as they incessantly take to their social media profiles to broadcast their products, services, news and activities.

What these enterprises have in common is their realization that advertising on social media is not only more convenient and pocket-friendly, but also has more impact (in the long run) on revenue generation – which is the goal of any profit-driven enterprise.

Needless to say, the direct consequence of people spending more and more time behind their phones (the average person spends <u>two hours and 15 minutes</u> every day on social media), as is the case nowadays, is that less and less time is left to spend watching television, and the advertisements airing on it.

To place a number to the assertion, people have been <u>found</u> in recent times to spend fifteen more minutes on social media than watching TV. In contrast, ads placed on social media are getting more views and engagements, as the ever burgeoning online environment continues to grow.

As a result, more brands are accepting social media marketing as an alternative to traditional marketing; a decision which daily statistics continue to prove right. Talking about statistics, social media marketing <u>was found</u> to gulp an incredible 11.7% of marketing budgets in the year 2016, with spending on social ads projected to hover around $30 billion that year.

As maddening as it may seem, this whopping sum is not uncalled for, as about 90% of all marketers who engage in social advertising admit that the venture has increased their brand's exposure.

The reasons why social media is becoming the advertising agency of choice for ad placers are not far-fetched; one of such reasons, which happens to be the most important to consider, is that social media ads reach consumers on a deep, personal level.

This is so because users, whose profile information is a great reveal of their behaviors and interests, can be better targeted by ads of products they already love, as opposed to advertisers scrambling for their choice audience through local television or search engines.

Another factor boosting the social marketing trend is that brands which advertise on social media platforms such as Facebook, Twitter and Instagram can, through posting their content, understand their customers better, and learn to advertise improve content – all the while maintaining a good relationship with them.

CHAPTER 1: THE WORLD OF FACEBOOK ADVERTISING

Why Facebook?

In its press release of April 25, 2018, Facebook announced that it had made about $12 billion in the first quarter of the year ending March 31st – an outstanding feat by a social media enterprise, "despite facing important challenges", as put forward by its founder and CEO, Mark Zuckerberg.

A colossal 91% of that revenue was due, in fact, to advertising, growing by 50% from around $7.8 billion realized in 2017.

Apart from revenue, the press release also placed the number of daily active subscribers somewhat around 1.45 billion, a 13% increase compared to what it was in the first quarter of the preceding year; and a similar increase in the number of monthly active subscribers which was recorded to kick at 2.2 billion.

Now get out of your goosebumps for a moment and ponder over these numbers; if Facebook can maintain anywhere close to this level of growth, then, in ten years, as fictitious as it sounds, a content placed on Facebook would reach half the world's population directly and through peer-to-peer interactions.

Facebook has enjoyed an unprecedented growth rate in the last few years, an expansion rate unrivalled and unchallenged by any of its contemporaries-cum-competitors; which has made it the biggest and most popular social networking platform in the world. Because of its sheer vastness, advertisers broadcasting on Facebook's virtual environment are apt to reach a considerably larger audience that would be possible via any other social route.

Therefore, as far as digital marketing is concerned, if it's going to be on social media at all, then it's better nowhere else but on Facebook.

Below are some reasons why advertising on Facebook is the absolute best choice you could make.

- **Largest social media outlet:** Without a shred of doubt, Facebook is the world's biggest arena for socializing on the internet, hosting around a quarter of the world's population on its pages.

- **Targeting:** Facebook is essentially a networking medium which allows users to share information about themselves on their profiles. This personal information such as likes, interests, hobbies, location, workplace, education, ethnicity, languages, behaviors and activities can be used by marketers to target specific kinds of people that they want their ads to reach.

  Post engagements are far more likely to happen when content is advertised to people who are interested in it.

- **Fortifying relationships:** Nothing is more important to a seller than making sales, and an important factor in the sales process is the marketer-consumer relationship.

Because consumers generally want to feel valued, heard, and cared for, a marketer or brand can easily have a direct interaction with their fans and consumers alike via their Facebook profile, thereby building trust and a long lasting relationship.

- **Cost of running ads:** The cost of setting up a Facebook ad campaign is relatively low, and not to forget that setting up a business page can be done at absolutely no cost.

- **Fair play:** Facebook offers all marketers a level playing field to reach as many targets as they want or can afford. This means small enterprises and startups can compete comfortably with the big brands and large corporations.

- **Simplicity and flexibility:** As immensely intricate as the Facebook marketing architecture is, the social media giant has, through the use of the best digital marketing technology available, made it incredibly easy to navigate through the processes of setting up and displaying ads, thereby extricating advertisers from having to reach out to the help center for support in every step.

In addition to this, marketers can tweak the ad campaign settings including targeting options, budget and schedule, as they like to ones that serve their purposes better.

- **The future shines great:** If stats-in-hand and past trends are anything to go by, then the average Facebook marketer should smile bright. Not only does Facebook advertising bring success in the present, they also hold great prospects for success in the nearby and distant future.

- **A road well-travelled:** Advertising on social media has come to stay. Since February 2018, the number of users advertising on Facebook has increased by 25 percent to around two-and-half million. And it can only grow.
- **Market guarantee:** It would be surprising, if not utterly shocking, if out of its 2.2 billion users, there are personality types that are not present on Facebook.

This is a form of well-packaged guarantee for marketers, who ought to be aware that no matter what their businesses are there are people who are interested in them, all that needs to be done is find them; and with proper targeting, Facebook has made this easy too.

- **Influence on buying decision:** Research has proved that Facebook influences users' decision to purchase products.

  Users are more likely to go ahead and check out a product if that product has been viewed, liked or shared by their friends.

  Facebook strategically lets a user know if a particular product in an ad has been liked by one or some of his friends, thus influencing their decision to check it out.

- **Measuring success:** Finally, when the plans are rolled out and ad campaigns set in motion, Facebook allows advertisers to track the success of their marketing schemes, by providing information on the number of impressions, likes, clicks and conversions that ads garner during the advertisement period.

Facebook has become the cornerstone of the social media arena, and as it continues to grow and increase in structural complexity, it's prudent for business owners to leverage on its immeasurable range of utility in order to drive traffic, make sales, create a fan base, and become popular and relevant in their respective industries. And there is no better way to achieve these than paid advertising.

ABC of Facebook advertising: understanding Facebook ads

Whatever the brand, whether it's a small coffee shop or a multinational automobile company, chances are there are tons of unique ad types and styles by way of which every brand can broadcast its content to customers in an effective and responsive manner. While there are a myriad of Facebook ads each serving specific purposes and exhibiting peculiar features, the major aim of an ad of whatever kind is to solicit a response from its viewer.

This response can exist in the form of making a purchase, visiting a website (traffic driving), or simply liking a page.

Facebook ads are designed in different formats and styles in order to suit the different needs of advertisers and requirements of products. It has been discovered that some ad types thrive better and make more conversions for a particular product than some others.

For example, while a blog would typically require a Link Click Ad to display its content and call to action, an e-commerce store would do better with the Carousel Ad type, which allows several products to be displayed in a single ad unit.

While advertisers have used several kinds of Facebook ads from their debut in users' news feeds in 2013 to effectively achieve their advertising objectives, it's expedient to understand that to achieve any form of success in digital marketing, not only does the right creative need to be served to targets, but also the proper ad type.

An understanding of what to use a particular ad type for, its advantages, limitations and demerits, will allow for a well-informed decision on choosing what type of ads to use in boosting that brand or driving that traffic.

A necessary breakdown of ad types served by Facebook is done below;

- **Link Click Ads (Domain Ads)**: These types, also called Page Post Link ads, are probably the most commonly used Facebook ads. With these ads, a brand can promote its external website by sending targets to its landing page or blog posts.

  Typically placed in the right column of the advertising page, they are essentially single image ads, allowing an optional text to be placed above, and an external website link below, the image, per ad unit.

  An important advantage of this ad type is that it allows users to engage with the brand's Facebook page, by either liking it, or sharing its content.

The specifications for Link Click ads are so set that the image is advisably 1200 by 628 pixels, Ad copy text is 90 characters long, headline and link description are 25 and 30 characters long, respectively.

A cornerstone of the Link Click ad type is that targets who visit an advertised website via the link can be tracked and retargeted on Facebook at a later date.

- **Offer Ads**: This ad type should be used to function as a standalone or in collaboration with the Link Click ads.

  They are used to target targets who are already familiar with the advertised brand, such as people who have visited its website and fans of its Facebook page. Offer ads lure visitors to a brand's site or blog by offering coupon codes or discounts which are traditionally tagged with an expiration date. This marketing trick is very apt to drive sales within the preset time.

- **Video Ads**: Like the Link Click ads, Facebook video ads can be utilized for both brand exposure and retargeting purposes.

The difference that split both ad formats apart is that instead of pictures, video ads broadcast videos to targets.

While the specified limit of uploaded video is set at over 90 minutes, most top performing video ads are usually less than a minute long. And why not? Nobody wants to be bored by exhaustingly long videos!

- **Multi-product Ads (Carousel Ads)**: These are especially pertinent to e-commerce brands who wish to promote a number of products to the same audience.

In the Carousel ad format, Facebook allows advertisers to place up to ten creatives (photos, videos, or a mix of both) in a single ad unit.

Brands using Carousel ads are privy to information on which advertised products get the most clicks, and Facebook automatically optimizes the ads so that the products with the most clicks appear first.

- **Lead Ads**: Lead ads are the perfect means of collecting leads or customers' information without having to leave the Facebook environment. The collected leads can be further used for retargeting.
- **Sponsored Posts**: These are basically usual Facebook posts that are boosted to reach more

people. The posts, like any other ads, can be targeted to reach specific audiences.

Because of the limiting effects of Facebook algorithm, posts by brands no longer reach the number of people they used to; such that no matter how large the fan base of a brand is, its posts would have to be amplified through paid advertisement for them to reach a majority or the entirety of the brand's followers.

- **Sponsored mentions**: Successful e-commerce stores can have an influence on buyers' decisions to buy from other stores.

That is why, through sponsored mentions, a brand can 'tag' itself with another brand while advertising its content.

The tagged brand is called an influencer, which, as its name suggests, is likely to influence a buyer's purchase decision.

- **Dynamic Product Ads (Dynamic Ads)**: Facebook's Dynamic ads can be used to display products (or products similar to the ones) customers have bought, added to their carts, or checked out.

  By way of this method, a brand can timely and effectively market and re-market products to customers who are actually interested in them, thereby fattening its chances of making sales.

- **Canvas Ads**: Canvas ads are a way of displaying multiple creatives (e.g. photos) in an interactive setup, such that viewers can easily swipe through and make adjustments (like zooming in and out and rotating) to them as they wish. Canvas ads are especially useful for displaying contents that are appreciated better in three dimensional views – like dresses and beauty products.

- **Collection Ads**: This ad type allows brands to showcase their products in a combined video-photo collage, enabling viewers to rummage through large numbers of the brands' commodities without having to visit their websites. Collection type ads are most suitable for marketing e-commerce brands.

- **Page Post Ads**: These ads can be used by a brand to engage its page fans. They could take the form of text, photos or videos, whichever is more appropriate for the content being advertised. An advantage of page post ads is that people engaging with them can be tracked and re-targeted with other ads.

- **Mobile App Ads**: As the name suggests, mobile app ads are functionally designed to drive targets to install a brand's mobile app(s).

  They are usually featured on Facebook mobile news feeds, and upon clicking on them, users are redirected to the app store where they can install the app. These ad formats have been recorded to command a high conversion rate.

- **Event and Local Awareness Ads**: Event ads are used by advertisers to broadcast an offline event they will be hosting.

  Depending on needs, these ads could be targeted to focus on people living within the locale of the advertised event. In contrast, local awareness ads are used to drive traffic to an offline store where people can make purchase.

Facebook ads are a great way of amplifying content to reach tons of people. When done ineffectively however, these ads could range from being a total waste of time and money to an utter disaster, and can even ruin a brand's name and integrity.

It's important to realize therefore, that while some ad types thrive well in marketing certain products, some others fail woefully in advertising same products, but are rather suited to advertising certain other products.

Making the choice of what ad formats to choose for our products can be enormously daunting, but with the proper guide this process is rendered ridiculously simple.

Why ads thrive on Facebook

Going by available, it's safe to say that Facebook ads are on steroids – and they will be for a long time.

The number of advertisers on the social media platform has doubled and tripled in the last few years, so much that we fear in a number of years the platform may become too congested with ads that unsponsored content would struggle for space in users' news feed.

This is a situation that is not peculiar to Facebook, but every other big-name social media outlet. But what has made paid advertisement so successful on social media? What is the secret formula?

Relevance is the key word. Ads on social have become increasingly relevant to the people they are designed to reach.

This is made possible by the sheer immensity of personal information that users make available in their online profiles. This information is stored by the social platform developers and stowed away for further use.

On request, this data is made available to advertisers who use it at will for their marketing purposes. This chain of reactions makes it possible for content advertisers to specifically target their preferred audience, thereby increasing their ads' chances of success.

No social platform employs this method of systematic data logging better than Facebook. It's no accident that the social giant made over ninety percent of its 2018 first quarter revenue from paid advertising.

Through the use of finely crafted ad formats, digital marketers have evolved from displaying annoyingly bland ads to showcasing brilliantly expressed content that viewers can simply no longer ignore.

CHAPTER 2: CREATING FACEBOOK ADS

Is Facebook advertising right for your business?

Whether it is confectionery products or designer clothing, fitness equipment or detox herbs, chances are there are hundreds and thousands of people out there who'd be interested in your product. And if they're out there, it's safe to assume that they are on Facebook. And why not, since the social giant hosts a quarter of the world's population.

Millions of businesses the world over are adopting digital advertising as an alternative to traditional means, and at the top of the digital advertising hierarchy is social media – and ultimately Facebook

– marketing. However, perhaps due to the level of ad technology currently in use at Facebook (which by the way is the most advanced on the web!), available ad designs and placements, not all businesses can make headway in Facebook marketing.

Before you decide to kick start an ad campaign for your brand, take some time to ask yourself some of the following real life questions, which have been tested to save you both time and currency.

- **Is your product geared towards fulfilling a particular interest?**

Whatever product you're aiming to promote, you need to be absolutely certain that it caters for a specific interest of Facebook users. This enables you to target those people who are likely to be interested in your product; the higher the number of people interested in your ad, the longer would be its reach.

- **Does your product have a demographic fine-tuning?**

Some products, such as fashion and beauty commodities, real estate properties, and automobiles, are typically targeted at people of a specific gender, age group, or cultural orientation.

- **Is your product limited to a particular location?**

If your product is available only in specific offline locations – such as malls or shops – then you would have to conduct a search of people living near you, because they are your most likely customers.

- **Was your product advertised, or is still being advertised, on another platform?**

Chances are if you have run a successful ad campaign via a platform other than Facebook (like Google AdWords), you'd be equally, or even more, successful in paid Facebook advertising.

This is so because Facebook offers better opportunities for ads to thrive – for much cheaper too – than on any other platform.

Answering "yes" to any of the questions above means that your product would most likely have a target audience on Facebook, and thus, is likely to be successful.

But in case you've been thrown in doubt by our well examined questions, here are some reasons why we think no matter what your doubts are, you should take that jump to join over 2 million others, into the sea of Facebook advertising:

1. Facebook's reach

This is a no-brainer. Facebook hosts somewhat around 2 billion users on a monthly basis, an audience that cuts across most known demographics and locations.

That's more than a fourth of the world's population which can be reached by ads of products they could be interested in.

In a recently released statistic, Facebook users were found to spend more time on the platform than they do watch television, meaning that you can place an ad on the platform and rest assured that your ad will be served to its intended target audience.

2. Powerful targeting

Facebook has the most targeting options available on the web. This is acquired from years of data collection from users all over the world.

When users share personal information such as their daily activities, the brands of clothes and jewelries they wear, their preferred books, educational and cultural background, location, workplace, behaviors, best movies and favorite singers, Facebook stores that information and makes it available for advertisers who can then leverage on it to find the best audience for their products and/or services.

3. Immediate results

Advertisers have recorded results of their Facebook ad campaigns within the first 2 to 3 days of setting them up, results which could have been rather impossible in such a short time without Facebook's effective ad schemes.

With the right strategies such as the ones demonstrated in this book, these immediate results are not only possible, but also guaranteed.

4. Remarketing and retargeting

Facebook has the capability to track its users' activities around the web, including what products they check out or purchase.

When such users log out of the websites on which they bought or viewed items, those items can be advertised and retargeted at these users through the Facebook retargeting program.

5. Goal-focused ad campaigns

Facebook ads are designed to be goal-driven, that is, geared towards achieving specific goals and objectives.

In earlier sections we mentioned some of these objectives – link clicks, video views, post engagement, website conversions, lead generation, and so on – and how and when they should be used.

With respect to the goals you want your ads to accomplish, you can use several ad types and designs to achieve your desired results. If your brand is an e-commerce business, for instance, you could use the carousel ad type to beautifully lay out your products in front of your audience.

Say you're into eBook marketing instead, then the link click ad type might just do it for you. Whatever the goals you set out to achieve with your advertising campaigns, you can rest certain that you have the best tools and services on the web to achieve them.

We'll discuss more on ad campaigns in the sections that follow.

6. Lead generation

Through Facebook's lead generation service, a brand can collect valuable information (including, but not limited to, names and email addresses) of its potential customers, and use same for remarketing and retargeting purposes.

7. The more-for-less paradox

You can reach more people on Facebook than on any other advertising platform, and for much less than you would spend on those platforms.

The typical cost of a thousand ad impressions on Facebook is 25 cents, an amount three times less than the nearest cost of getting same on another digital marketing platform, LinkedIn.

Facebook presently offers the most advanced digital ad technology, and is keen on keeping ahead of others in the game by adding several new features and functionalities every now and then.

All this, while maintaining the lowest price per ad impression you can find anywhere. So if you're thinking of reaching out to more people with that product or hot idea of yours, then Facebook is your best bet on the adventure.

Choosing the right marketing objective

The previous chapter analyzes the different ad formats, their features and how they should be used to achieve resounding success in digital advertising.

After making its choice of ad format, a brand might be faced by another challenge: the "What do I want viewers to do with my ad?" question pops up, and as easy as it seems, it has the potential to lead to the success or downfall of an ad campaign.

Because most advertisers are primarily interested in driving traffic to their websites, it's customary to find them attaching external web links to all their ads. And most times it works too!

A brand can make sales, collect leads, create awareness and drive traffic all in one ad campaign; that's like killing several birds almost without aiming.

However, this tactic is very often overused; and once that is done, it becomes difficult for such brands to get positive results from their advertising. Viewers are not to be bored with monotonous ads, else they would add such erring brands to their mental blacklist.

While some ads can be used to drive traffic and make sales, some others should be used mainly to solicit engagements or create awareness. That is to say, a mix of several ad objectives need to be employed in order for a brand to keep its audience clicking.

A marketing objective is the action an advertised content requests from its viewers. Quite rightly, setting an objective is the first step in the ad campaign formation process.

At present, there are a total of 14 different campaign objectives on Facebook from which an advertiser can choose. A knowledge of what these campaign objectives are and when to use them is paramount in the marketing procedure.

Facebook has created three categories under which all the different campaign objectives fall. They are Awareness, Consideration and Conversion. Let's dive in and expound each of them.

Awareness

There are three campaign objectives under the Awareness category – Brand Awareness, Local Awareness, and Reach.

- **Brand Awareness**: The brand awareness objective is used to create awareness about a brand and to increase its popularity.

    Brand awareness ads are usually targeted at people who are very likely to pay attention to them.

    Because these ads are exclusively dedicated to creating awareness and not in driving traffic or making sales, they offer a very narrow range of possibilities for small businesses; hence, they are often employed by high-earning brands.

- **Local Awareness**: This marketing objective is engaged when an ad is to be created solely to reach targets near a local (offline) business.

  Ads carrying this objective have limited targeting options, since only people near the geographic location of the advertised brand are usually in focus. These ad types are not suitable for small brands.

- **Reach**: This is probably the best awareness campaign objective for small businesses. With the reach objective, an ad is set to reach the maximum number of people for the set budget.

  This makes it easy for a brand with a small fan base to reach out all of the people in its audience in a single ad campaign.

Consideration

The Consideration category is the most vast in the number of objective options it offers. Under it are camped the following ad objectives:

- **Traffic**: As the name suggests, this ad objective is used to drive traffic to from Facebook to an external website. It is probably the most frequently used – and abused – campaign objective.

  Used appropriately, ads featuring this objective can successfully increase a brand's popularity in the virtual world.

- **Engagement**: The Engagement ad campaign objective is further subdivided into four types:

  o **Post Engagement**: The Post Engagement objective should be used for a content that is already doing well in terms of engagement, which an advertiser wants to boost.

- **Page Likes**: This is basically employed for ads that are soliciting page likes on Facebook. They tend to increase a brand's fan base.

- **Event Responses:** This objective should be used to amplify events created on Facebook, which targets would be requested to attend.

- **Offer Claims**: A campaign objective used while specifically broadcasting offers on purchases, such as discounts and coupons.

- **App Installs**: Nobody wants their apps to gather dust on the shelves of their virtual stores.

Therefore, advertisers looking to get downloads for their software should use this objective to create ads requesting viewers to install their app.

- **Video Views**: Like the App Installs objective, the Video Views campaign objective is used get viewers to view created videos.

  Due to its low cost and the teeming popularity of videos as an advertising content, this campaign objective is recommended for brands aiming to market their video content.

- **Lead Generation**: The last of the Consideration ad campaign objectives is Lead Generation. Leads can be obtained from Facebook users through lead ads which traditionally make offers – such as sign-ups for newsletters – via links attached to an advertised content.

When users click on this link, they are directed to a page where they are required to provide their details (typically name and email address). This information can then be stored and used for other purposes.

The entirety of the lead generation process is made easier by Facebook, as sign forms are auto-filled from information already available on the platform.

This essentially makes lead generation a two-click process; opening the form page with one click, and submitting the auto-filled form with another.

Conversion

There are three campaign objectives under the Conversion category.

- **Conversions**: The Conversions objective should be used to drive people to an external site on which they are required to take specific actions, such as making a purchase, signing up for newsletters, or sharing a blog post.
- **Product Catalog Sales**: This campaign objective is very often utilized by e-commerce brands who want to market and remarket products to customers who have viewed them, or viewed similar products.

After a customer buys a product, adds it to his cart, or simply views it on a brand's website, the product (and similar products) are added to the brand's catalog, from where they are automatically retargeted at the people who have engaged with them.

- **Store Visits**: The Store Visits objective is functionally similar to the Local Awareness objective, the important difference being that while the Local Awareness campaign objective should be used to create awareness about one shop location, the Store Visits objective is usually used to advertise multiple business locations.

Choosing a campaign objective is unarguably the cornerstone of digital advertising, for not only is an ad campaign predisposed to being successful with the right one, but is also apt to fail miserably with the wrong one.

Choosing ad placements, budget and schedule

Ad placements

The various platforms and environments on which an ad is placed to run are called placements.

Depending on the choice of campaign objective and the content being advertised, an ad can be run on the myriad of Facebook outlets, including the Facebook app, Messenger, Instagram, and other Facebook-affiliated applications and websites.

As at this moment there are a total of thirteen placement options under four platforms, on which Facebook ads can be run. These platforms are Facebook, Instagram, Messenger and Audience Network.

Facebook

- **Facebook Feeds**: This placement option allows ads to be shown on users' desktop news feeds (for users accessing Facebook with their desktop, mac or laptop computers) or mobile news feeds (for users using the Facebook mobile app or accessing Facebook via a mobile browser), or a combination of both.

  While majority of ads can be run on both desktop and mobile news feeds, sometimes an ad requires users to take complicated steps or visit 'heavy websites' which are better accessed on desktop; in this case, it's advisable to target such ad to desktop users only.

- **Right Column**: In this placement ads are run on the right columns of the Facebook platform, and only visible to desktop users.
- **Instant Articles**: ads can also be fashioned to run in Instant Articles, a tool designed to run on the Facebook mobile app via which content creators can share interactive articles with their readers. An important point to note is that ads running in Instant Articles must be placed in Mobile News Feed as well.
- **In-stream Video**: Through this outlet, ads are embedded as short videos within Facebook's Live video and Video on Demand.
- **Suggested Videos**: When users view a video on Facebook, they are exposed to more

'suggested videos' which they can view as well. Ads can be sandwiched between these suggested videos.

- **Marketplace**: This is a relatively new placement medium at the moment. Marketplace is an arena for buying and selling on Facebook.

Ads running in Marketplace appear when users enter Marketplace in the Facebook mobile app. For an ad to be run in Marketplace, it must have the Reach, Traffic, Conversions, Catalog sales or Video views objective.

Instagram

Although not as successful as on Facebook, ads on Instagram have been recorded to boost sales and achieve high ROIs.

Because Instagram is primarily a visuals platform (showcasing photos and videos), advertisers looking to run ads on it must be able to create streams of content that are both appealing to see and suitable to the environment. Instagram advertisers are provided with two options of ad placements to choose from, Feeds and Stories.

- **Instagram Feeds**: Ads placed here appear on users' desktop and mobile feeds.
- **Stories**: Stories are a great way for people to share personal experiences and activities on Instagram. Ads can be placed in Instagram stories.

Messenger

Facebook Messenger has been introduced to the world of digital marketing, allowing advertisers to reach the 1.3 billion people who use the elite messaging app.

Ads in Messenger should have the Traffic, Conversions, App installs, Reach, Messages, Brand awareness, or Catalog sales objective, and can be placed in either the Messenger home tab or sponsored messages.

- **Home**: Ads are displayed in Messenger's home tab.
- **Sponsored Messages**: Here, ads are delivered as direct messages to people already in conversation with the advertiser.

Audience Network

Ads placed in Audience Network reach people outside of the Facebook platform.

These ads are placed on certain websites, mobile apps and TV apps associated with Facebook. The three ad types placed on Audience Network are:

- **Native, banner and Interstitial**: Image and video ads are displayed in this format.
- **In-stream videos**: Ads can be displayed to people while watching videos outside Facebook.
- **Rewarded videos**: Ads can also be displayed as rewarded videos, which are full-screen videos offered to viewers in exchange for a reward.

Facebook offers two methods of selecting these ad placements, automatic and manual.

Automatic placement: Using this approach, ads are broadcasted automatically on such platforms as would optimize campaign results.

Placements which perform better for an ad are allocated more of the campaign budget than others, thereby ensuring that the advertised content hits the maximum reach attainable by the preset budget.

Though the cost per ad delivery varies across the different placements, the automatic placement method ensures that ads get the lowest overall cost per ad optimization event. This is the recommended ad placement method by Facebook.

Manual placement: If for some reason you find the automatic placement method unappealing, ineffective, or simply not suitable for the ad variety, then you can select the manual placement method to showcase your ads.

As per Facebook's recommendations in the placement context, an advertiser should choose more than one placement for effective running of ads.

The combinations of placements for various ad campaign objectives are:

- **Brand awareness**: Facebook and Instagram
- **Video views**: Facebook, Instagram and Audience Network
- **Engagement**: Instagram and Facebook

- **App Installs**: Facebook, Instagram, Audience Network and Messenger
- **Traffic**: Facebook, Messenger and Audience Network
- **Conversions**: Facebook, Instagram and Audience Network

Setting a campaign budget

Whether it's to make sales, drive traffic or create awareness, the ultimate goal of all Facebook ads – or at least a vast majority of them – is revenue generation, directly (like getting customers to make purchases) or indirectly (such as driving traffic to a website where they can learn about products).

While there are a number of factors responsible for the success or downfall of any campaign, budget is perhaps the most powerful influencer of an ad's revenue generation curve.

Before you embark on your budgeting journey, it's important to have a knowledge of the costs of setting up ads on Facebook.

Though several factors – such as placements, targeted country, offer, and ad design – can affect the costs of setting up ads, the cost-per-click of Facebook ads continues to hover around $1.

Bearing this in mind, a potential advertiser can design a well-informed scheme of expenditures vis-à-vis expected revenue for a particular campaign.

While this might seem simple, it'll amaze you how many ads fail due to inadequate planning, or total lack thereof. Since so much hinges on budgeting, it's important therefore to optimize the process, so that ad expenses are neither unbearable nor inadequate.

The first step towards choosing the right budget for a campaign is to lay out a campaign goal. This is as easy as it sounds – knowing (and laying forth) the objective of an ad campaign, whether it's product sales, lead generation, video views, or post engagement on a message.

It is pertinent to set a campaign goal because it allows the advertiser to make important management decisions, such as how much would be required to achieve the set goal, and how much time the campaign would have to last for.

After setting a campaign goal, the next step is to start working backwards from the final step of the campaign process to the primordial step. For instance, say a brand wants to make $10,000 in eBook sales via advertising within a month, if one eBook costs $10, then it'll have to make 1,000 sales to arrive at the target revenue.

To make that number of sales, 1,000 customers would have to buy an eBook each. If the ad has an estimated conversion rate of 20% (2 in every 10 people or leads that come across the ad would make a purchase), then the ad would need to get about 5,000 leads.

To get the number of leads highlighted above from a campaign, the audience size would have to be significant – larger than 5,000.

Calculating the ideal audience size for our ads can be daunting and tricky, because the reach of Facebook ads depends on several factors, including the schedule of the ads, duration, and availability of target audience during the length of the campaign. To get an ad to perform optimally in light of these variables, meticulous planning is required. And it is not rocket science.

A basic knowledge of your audience is crucial in any ad campaign you are going to put up. If you have an active target audience, then you'd expect them to turn up on Facebook at least once in a week; for a not-so-active audience group, that time might stretch to a month.

Nevertheless, average Facebook users log into their accounts at least once in three months, and that's why your ad set should be set to last for that long, at least.

But even if your target audience logs into the platform often and your campaign is set to run for half a year, how certain can you be that Facebook would serve your ads to them? This exhumes to light another issue: Facebook ads bidding.

The assumption that an ad placed on Facebook would most certainly get shown to its target audience couldn't be farther from the truth.

Because Facebook is caught between serving advertisers (by delivering their ads to target audiences) and providing the best experience for its users, it introduced the ads bidding process to enable it deliver the most relevant content to users.

Three factors influence the delivery of an ad, the ad campaign bid, ad relevance score, and estimated ad action rates. The bidding process is designed to mimic and auction, such that when an auction happens, all three aforementioned factors are integrated and standardized into a single total value.

The ad with the highest total value is crowned winner and thus shown to its target audience. So in order to beat this obstacle, we advise that you always bid the highest that you think an ad campaign is worth – not overbidding, or more dangerously, underbidding.

Still walking the path of our example, the next step in line would be to calculate your ad's impression count, and to do this, we'll use ad frequencies.

Ad frequency is the number of times an ad gets served to a viewer. If in the three months our ad example above is set to run for it gets viewed ten times by each target, then our impression count should be somewhere around 50,000 (number of leads multiplied by ad frequency). This ad impression count is important in determining the CPM (Cost Per Thousand) of the campaign, which is how much the impression count would cost you.

CPM can vary, depending on competition, audience's location, ad type, and the chosen ad objective.

In our example, we're using the website conversions campaign objective, which should have a CPM of $(10 – 12)$. After arriving at a CPM, the next and final step is to calculate the cost per ad set.

This is pretty straightforward and doesn't take a lot of math skills, just multiply the estimated ad impression count by the obtained CPM, then divide the result by 1,000.

In our example, this would be 50,000 multiplied by $(10 - 12)$, which gives $500,000 - $600,000, and divided by 1,000 we get $500 to $600. This is our ad budget, which is approximately the cost of making $10,000 in eBook sales from the conversion of 5,000 leads into 1,000 sales, while assuming a conversion rate of 20%.

This is the budget per ad set, and as every ad campaign would usually feature more than one ad set, budget for all ad sets should be calculated in this manner and summed up to arrive at a total campaign budget.

It should be noted that the ideal conversion rate is not arrived at by assumption as we had done, but through a formula: the percentage of people who click on an ad upon viewing it multiplied by the percentage of people who buy the product upon clicking on the ad. It is therefore precautionary to opt for a much lower conversion rate, typically below 10%, so as to arrive at a realistic budget.

Choosing a delivery schedule for your ads

There have been several debates over the best times to deliver Facebook ads to users. One school of thought states that it's probably best to place them on weekends, another stating that weekdays are more likely to produce results.

While there might be some bases for both points of view, the latter might actually have more bone to its flesh of reason. The reason is, according to research, posts are likely to get the highest click-through rates on Wednesday around 3pm, and, going by the same source, the worst times to post are on weekends. However blunt these statistics choose to be, we advise that they best times to post on Facebook depends on a group of factors.

First, knowledge of the behaviors of the target audience is helpful in determining when best to put an ad in from of it. For instance, if an ad is targeted at users aged between 30 and 45, then it's safe to assume that they would be at work on weekday afternoons and immersed in their beds on weekend mornings.

While at work, ads of interest seen by a target could be shared with co-workers who in turn might share with their friends and families, ultimately leading to a decent return on investment. It'll makes sense therefore, to post such ads to this working class during times when they are most likely to respond. In another scenario, imagine an ad about *potty* training targeted at mothers of kids aged between a month and 3 years. These mothers may be best served on weekend evenings when they have time to think about things other than their kids and day jobs.

Judging from the examples given above, we can further add concrete to our earlier assertion that the behaviors and lifestyle of target audiences are the major determiners of the optimal time to schedule a post.

However indifferent we might be apt to get here, it's important to point out that there are some constants which are liable to affect an advertising campaign, such as the so-called "paycheck effect" – which invariably makes consumer spending escalate in the beginning and middle of the month. Another constant that keeps popping up is a statistic that favors Monday as the day when many online businesses record their highest number of sales, between 13:00 and 14:00.

If you own a business, then you do your own research to know when you make your most sales and when you make your least, down to the hour of the day. This record is especially helpful now that Facebook has made it possible to schedule ads to run at specific times of chosen days.

If you've run an ad campaign in the past or you still do, be it on Facebook or on any other platform, then you can tell when your ads experienced their highest engagements. If that ad campaign was successful then you could reuse that schedule to run your new ads.

However, if you haven't been engaged in an ad campaign prior to this moment, then we recommend taking a glance at the various researches done on the subject matter to determine the best times to run your ads.

Hootsuite, for example, found the best times to post on Facebook to be between 12:00 and 15:00 on Mondays, Wednesdays, Thursdays, and Fridays; and between 12:00 and 13:00 on Saturdays and Sundays.

Another research by Coschedule confirms that posts get more clicks at 15:00 and more engagements at 13:00 on Thursdays, Fridays, Saturdays, and

Sundays. Keeping this in mind, you could opt to run link click ads at 15:00 and engagement-focused ads at 13:00. Also, know that these times may vary depending on who you're targeting.

If you're targeting businesses, then weekdays are most likely the best days to push your ads to them. Consumers, in contrast, have been found to have great engagement with ads on weekends.

Though proven to have positive impacts on the reception of ads, this dayparting manner of scheduling however, does have its drawbacks. In the traditional way Facebook schedules ads to run, ads are served to target audiences for the entire length of the day.

This way, more people are reached than would be reached if, say, those ads were scheduled to run only between 13:00 and 14:00. So bear in mind that while your ads might be better received during the times you have scheduled them to run on, they might also be reaching fewer people, and thus garnering less impressions than you would with Facebook's automatic scheduling.

It is imperative therefore, to take in all of the advice and recommendations given here and try to figure out what works for your business.

Choosing the optimum budget: the $1 rule versus the golden rule

Choosing a budget that's commensurate with the financial goal of your ad is without doubt the right thing to do; commensurate, in this sense, meaning that the ad spend is a fraction of the target revenue to accrue from such an ad. In the example given above, the estimated ad cost arrived at was $500, which was to secure the sales of 1,000 eBooks totaling $10,000 in revenue.

In this case, the total expenditure was just 5% of the target revenue. However, there are digital schools of thought that are of the opinion that a dollar a day is enough ad budget to cater for an average brand's advertising needs. Let's examine this assertion briefly.

According to the marketing and social media marketer, Brian Carter, it'd cost about $0.25 for an ad to get 1,000 impressions on Facebook; that is to say, 4,000 impressions are obtainable by an ad per dollar spent, and $30 to reach 120,000 people per month. This is by far a cheaper plan than one on any other advertising outlet in the world today, which is why it appeals greatly to startups and small businesses.

For a small brand, this is perhaps a buck-saving pathway to digital advertising success, a short-cut, if you like. But for a large business that wants to thrive in the face of major competitions, a little more financial extroversion is required.

This is not to discredit in any manner the essence of investing a dollar a day on Facebook ads. In fact, available <u>evidence</u> proves otherwise.

The golden rule however, states that advertisers should make their ad budget a sizeable percentage of their target revenue on that ad.

This is demonstrated in the example given above, in which case five percent of the total accruable revenue was expended. Still on our example, if $1 was spent a day for the three months our ad was to run for, then we would arrive at a total of $90 in budget. For that period.

This amount can only secure a fraction (less than a fifth) of the required impressions to land our target number of leads, and is ultimately insufficient in making our target number of sales.

The instance cited here holds true for all advertising campaigns that are geared towards reaching substantial milestones and staying afloat in a seemingly limitless sea of digital ads.

The world of Facebook advertising as we know it is a battleground where only the strongest survive. And just as one doesn't go to war with their weakest boots, a digital marketer can't afford to approach an advertising campaign with a groggy budget. This is the main idea of the golden rule.

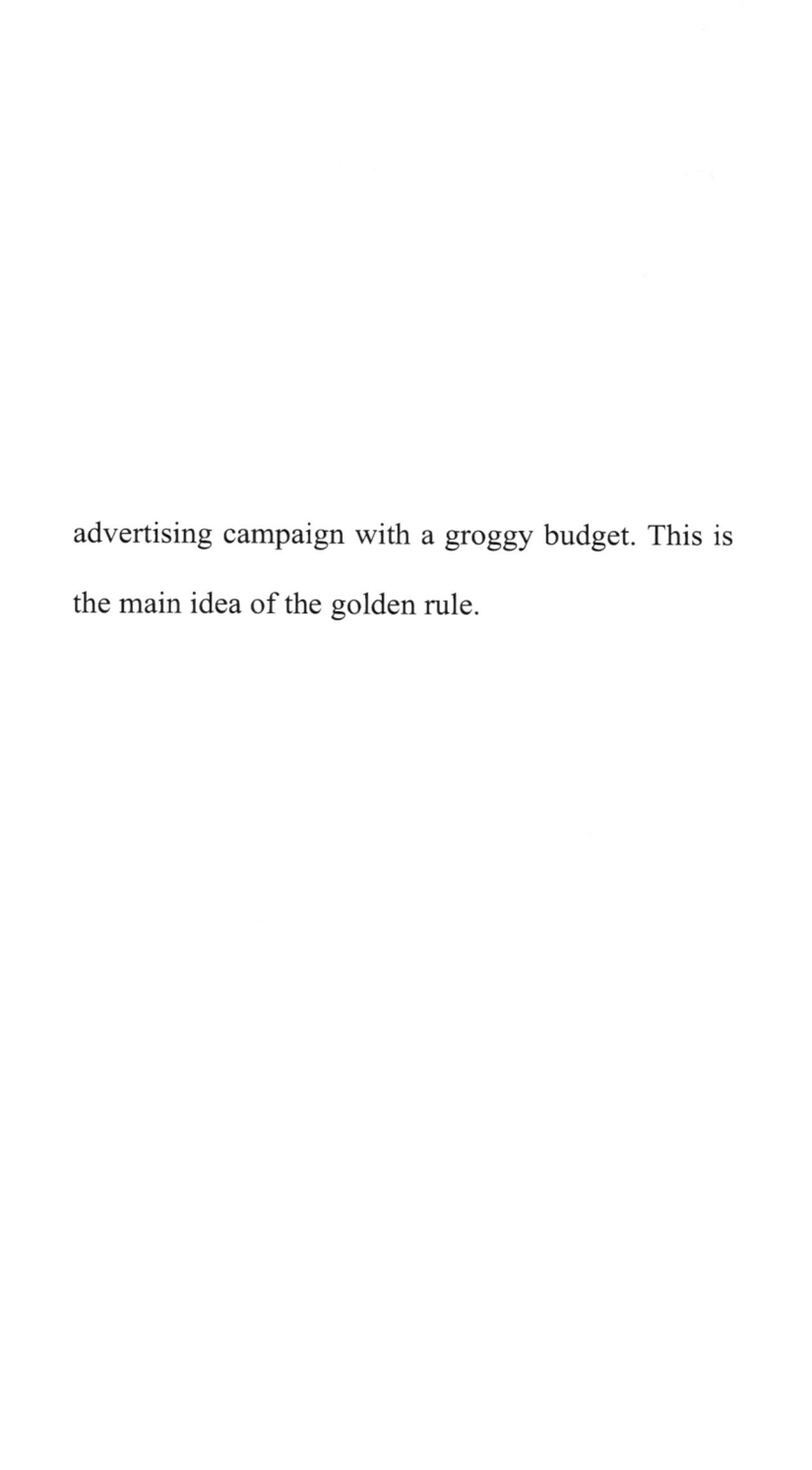

CHAPTER 3: TARGETING

Defining your audience

Before going on to find the people who are most likely to feed on your content, let's first go on a discourse to explain how Facebook targeting works.

When you view or buy a product on a website (such as an e-commerce store), the user's browser shares information about what you're looking at or purchasing with third-party advertising platforms – Facebook, in this case.

When you log into Facebook, the products you have viewed or bought might show up again, this time in your feed or right column (depending on what placement are set for the ads), being retargeted at you in hopes of drawing you back to the website; and with the kind of interest you had shown in the product, you might as well just purchase it.

Facebook offers two key options in targeting an audience: broad and specific targeting. In broad targeting, a group of desired audience characteristics or interests are selected, and people are added to their audience base if they match any of these interests.

For example, if you're broad targeting lovers of novels, documentaries and TV shows, then everybody who loves soccer would be added to your audience, as well as all the lovers of documentaries and those of TV shows.

That is to say, the audience grows larger with every interest included. In specific targeting however, the audience is narrowed down via the inclusion of more interests. If specific targeting were preferred in our example above, then the audience would be made up of people who exhibit all three interests, novels, documentaries and TV shows.

There are three known ways to accomplish specific targeting: layered targeting, custom audiences, or lookalike audiences.

In layered targeting, several characteristics or interests are merged together to narrow down and refine an audience base.

For example, an ad with layered targeting can be used to reach divorced home owners who live in North Carolina. With the custom audience setting, an advertiser can target people based on customer information (email addresses or phone numbers which would be uploaded), website traffic (which Facebook measures, thanks to the Facebook Pixel), app activity, and engagement (based on a list of people who engaged with content on Facebook or Instagram).

Lookalike audiences are users whose characteristics match those of an already created source audience. The degree to which lookalike audiences match the original audience can be set, in percentages, with smaller percentages depicting closer matching.

While either of the targeting options might be selected to reach the people of interested, it is worthy of note that the more specific you get while defining your audience, the higher your chances of making headway in that campaign. We recommend that advertisers take a cue from the following points in defining an ideal target audience.

- **Understand available ad targeting attributes**

Facebook offers four primary sets of attributes for targeting purposes: interest, location, demographics, and behaviors.

1. **Targeting based on interest**

Facebook interests allow targeting of people who are interested in a particular idea, product or service. When these interests are in line with or related to your products, you could target those people exhibiting them.

2. **Targeting based on location**

The location attribute is especially useful for creating awareness about local stores and country-specific products. Using this attribute, an advertiser can target people in and around a particular geographical area.

3. Targeting based on demographics

Facebook allows marketers to target people based on their age, gender, educational background, relationship status, and more. This further refines the process of setting up an audience that is most likely to respond to ads.

4. Targeting based on behaviors

Behavior targeting allows you to target people based on their habits and activities on the web. Behaviors such as purchasing products and playing online games, for instance, could be used by e-commerce stores and games developers to target people who are likely to patronize them.

- **Make use of data tools to best gather information about your audience**

There are various data collection tools designed and made available for marketing purposes; one of such tools is Facebook Audience Insights. You can feed into Insights your customers' email addresses or phone numbers to get information about their demographics and behaviors.

This information can then be used to properly target them with ads. More on the Audience Insights tool is given in later segments.

- **Build loyalty with existing fans and customers**

Apart from the glaring fact that Facebook offers the best advertising experience on the web for digital marketers, it also offers them the best platform to interact with, and grow solid relationships with, their loyal customers and fans.

Using a Facebook page, a brand can connect with people who have shown interest in its products and/or services by liking its page, and it should, since these people are most likely to drive sales.

No matter what targeting strategy you decide to utilize in your ad campaign, you should be objective enough to try to figure out which strategies work for a particular ad placement and which ones don't.

Facebook audience insights: doing a demographic research

Facebook Audience Insights is a powerful tool designed to help advertisers better target their chosen audiences by getting privy to information about them, including their demographics, location, and purchase behavior.

It's an important tool not only for advertising purposes, but also in gathering user data that can help in improving marketing strategies.

This data is obtained from two major sources: through users' self-posted data (which includes all information users post on the platform about themselves – such as age, location, gender, workplace, relationship status, job title, etc.) and through Facebook-affiliated data brokers. Facebook obtains people's data such as purchasing behavior from third-party companies who match that data to Facebook user IDs.

The Audience Insights tool is located in "Ads Manager" on the top left of the Ads Manager page. Once you click on this, you'll see the "All Tools" button on the bottom right of the Ads Manager tab.

From there, you'll see the Audience Insights button under the "Plan" category. This will take you to the main screen where you'll be introduced to the three different types of audiences, everyone on Facebook, people connected to your page, and a custom audience.

- **Everyone on Facebook**: This audience pathway gives information about all Facebook users in the target location of your choice.

- **People connected to your page**: This option gives information on people who are already connected to you via your page.

- **A custom audience**: A brand can set a custom audience by uploading people's phone numbers or email addresses, which Facebook would then match to existing user accounts. Using this audience type allows the brand to get valuable information about people who is already interested in it. If you install Facebook Pixel on your website, then you can create a custom audience of those users who are active on it.

Once an option has been selected, you'll be taken to a page that lays out information about your selected audience. You can then define the "seed" audience you want to analyze on that page by entering their location, demographics, and at least an interest.

You may also include other details such as their relationship status, home, education, life events, and political affiliations. Because the Insights page is interactive, information displayed would change every time the audience is refined or changed.

Still on the page, you can navigate to the page likes tab to see what pages your set audience have liked the most, and under what categories those pages fall.

The Insights tool has been hailed by some as the most important of marketing tools, and for good reason. The information obtainable from Audience Insights is invaluable in carrying out researches to determine the behaviors and attitudes of customers and potential customers alike.

Creating the ideal ad copy and image

Creating an ingenious product to sell to customers is great, but portraying it in a way that makes your customers want to buy is a totally different ball game.

Needless to say, you could have the best commodities out in the market, yet make very few sales because of the way you market them.

This is especially true with using the Facebook advertising platform, where your products are not physically available for inspection, so you'll have to rely on your creative to make sales.

Without any intention to scare anyone, it's safe to state that creating an ideal ad copy and image does not come easy – it's actually the opposite.

Ad copy

Writing a great ad copy is, as put by Facebook itself, is both a science and an art. Taking the guesswork out of an ad campaign is the dream of every marketer, and these tips are proven to help with just that.

- **Tailor your ad write-up to a particular audience:** An ad copy for an ad targeted at seniors, for example, should be written differently one meant for college students. The tone of voice you use is important here.
- **Put the most important words first**: Remember that your target audience is made up of people who are not primarily on Facebook to see ads. So make your message clear and

straight to the point. No need to beat about the bush, it's not fiction writing. Moreover, some of the last words in your copy might be truncated by Facebook, so make sure you get those convincing words out first.

- **The customer comes first**: You have to write as though you were in your audience's shoes. Appeal to their emotions and sentiments, share in their pains and glory; make yourself one of them, and you'll write better ad copies.

- **Write with consistency**: One of the reasons why the *James Bond* series sold out so much and garnered so many fans across the globe is the simple fact that the actors, no matter how many, all had similar attributes and took similar actions. People like consistency, so no matter how many ad copies you write, be sure to stay consistent in your choice of style and tone.

- **Include numbers:** If you ad is about offers or sales, make sure to include numbers, if you can. People want to know what they stand to gain from your ad right away, and there's no better way of telling them than including that "20% off" or "buy 2 get 1 free" line.

- **Match your ad copy to your visual:** Your copy needs to provide a smooth transition from text to image; trust me, your audience wouldn't want a bumpy ride in this one. Your message needs to reflect what your image portrays, else you offer a jarring experience for your viewers.

Ad image

Yes, you could go on a fly and download tons of stock images to use for your campaign, but what makes an image the right one for that campaign, or for a particular ad? Definitely not intuition.

You ad might escape death with a bad ad copy, but with the wrong image, it's certain to return far less than optimal results.

These tips would serve you right on your way to choosing your image of choice.

- **Make it unique:** This is where you have to be careful with stock images (sorry, Google). Consider a scenario where 2 million advertisers are trying to push their ads in front of users on the same platform, and imagine the tons of images they would need to do so. It's boring, you would agree, to have the see the same images used over and over again by different advertisers for different purposes.

Users want new, stand-out content they can relate with, so it's highly recommended that you come up with your own images.

- **Use colors:** One of the most effective ways to make your ad stand out in endless streams of visual data is an efficient mix of colors. Using bright, contrasting colors can help you to achieve this, and eliminate or alleviate the risk of people scrolling past your ad without paying it a glance.

- **Let your image dominate:** Using minimal text in your ad allows you to optimally utilize the space available for your creative. Since images are proven to be more successful than text in capturing attention, using little text increases your ad's chances of getting results.

Ad copies and images are the keys to unlocking your ads' world of possibilities. Therefore, care must be taken to exercise the right amounts of each, if your ads – and campaigns in general – are going to be a success.

Lead generation and conversion with Facebook ads

A lead is a person who, usually by way of submitting personal details such as email addresses or phone numbers, has indicated an interest in a product or service.

Your leads are the most likely people to patronize your products, hence why your retargeting ads might be solely focused on them. This is perhaps why 85% of marketers stated in a research that lead generation was a top priority in their advertising agenda.

Lead generation therefore, incorporates the processes involved in obtaining the aforementioned details from people, thereby converting them from total stranger into leads. As we have already discussed lead generation ads in earlier sections, we won't be delving further into that now. Rather, we'll give you a few tips and strategies for creating and nurturing leads.

- **Create offers and contests:** Contests and giveaways are a sure way to land leads. According to Unbounce, adding contests alone to their lead generation platforms boosted leads by up to 700%.

- **Create videos:** Using products explainer videos instead of mere text or image, a lead generation ad can be made to be more appealing to its viewers, landing leads at a rate of up to 33%.

- **Keep negative text at bay:** Negative words (such as "spam") has been found to affect lead generation campaigns badly, often decreasing its conversion rate.

- **Cut clicking options:** Be sure to minimize clicking options on the landing page of your lead generation campaign (and leave only the "Sign Up" button), as this is sure to reduce confusion thereon, thereby increasing conversion rate.

- **Enrich your website, blog, or landing page:** When leads land on your website – which is the dream of any lead generation marketer – one of the first things they are exposed to is the content of the page they've been directed to. A great strategy for nurturing leads is keeping them educated and fascinated with your content.

While lead generation and website conversion serve similar purposes, it is pertinent to not confuse the two disparate schemes. Lead generation is typically achieved via sign up forms placed on the Facebook platform; for website conversion however, sign up forms are located on the marketer's website.

But whatever your choice, either pathway would usually deliver similar results.

CHAPTER 4: CREATING A PROFITABLE FACEBOOK MARKETING CAMPAIGN

Setting a campaign goal

Choosing the right campaign goal or objective is critical to the overall success of the campaign. A Facebook campaign objective is the cornerstone of the overall campaign structure.

Every Facebook campaign should have a single objective and here is where a lot of Facebook advertisers get confused. A mistake Facebook advertisers often make while setting up a Facebook campaign is to choose the wrong campaign objective.

No matter how fascinating your ad copy and image is or how detailed your targeting is, if you choose the wrong objective then your campaign won't perform as well as expected.

While the different types of Facebook objectives have been explained in an earlier segment of this book, it is imperative that we give you the right perspective of what a campaign objective is.

Having people click on your sponsored posts in their hundreds and thousands is awesome, anyone would want that. However, tons of likes and comments on your post without any positive effect on your sales curve is a total waste – of time and money.

That is why, when setting up a campaign, the first question you need to ask yourself is: *why am I putting up this campaign?* This question is a sum total of the responsibility of that campaign, which could rightly be driving sales, landing leads, creating awareness, or post engagement.

It is right to assert that each campaign should only have one goal, which is the heartbeat of that marketing effort. Too many goals in an advertising campaign promotes confusion and inconsistency, two traits you are most likely to succeed without.

Measuring the impacts of your ads

No one wants to waste resources on social media advertising. If you place an ad on Facebook, chances are you hope to one day obtain a return on your investment. A positive ROI in your ad campaign proves that your advertising efforts are paying off, and that's good news to your bank account. But what is considered success, and how can you measure the impacts your ads are having on your business?

Measuring the impacts of your campaign requires a solid knowledge of the parameters that influence the health of your ads. These parameters are called metrics, and knowing what they are and how they affect your ads' heartbeat is all important in the impact measuring process.

Here is an explanation of the most relevant metrics used in calculating the success of an ad campaign.

- **COST PER ACTION (CPA)**: The ultimate goal is any ad is to garner certain actions from its viewers. These actions include page likes, video views, sign ups, sales, and app downloads. Cost per action is how much you're willing to pay for an action you want a target audience to take on your ad.

- **CLICK–THROUGH RATE (CTR)**: As the term suggests, click-through rate is the rate at which people are clicking on your ads upon viewing them. The average CTR in Facebook advertising across all industries is 0.9%.

- **COST PER THOUSAND IMPRESSIONS (CPM)**: This is the amount of money you have chosen to pay for Facebook to show your ads to your target audience one thousand times.

- **FREQUENCY**: Frequency is the number of times your ad is served to each person in your target audience. Mathematically, frequency is arrived at by diving the total number of impressions by the reach of your ad.

- **RETURN ON INVESTMENT (ROI)**: This is an obvious one. The primary aim of setting up ads, whatever the kind, is to make money directly (such as from sales) or indirectly (such as lead generation and website conversions).
- **RETURN ON AD SPEND (ROAS)**: ROAS measures the total revenue generated per unit of currency spent of advertising. It is mathematically equal to generated revenue divided by advertising spend.

Now that you have a fair knowledge of the metrics that affect your ads, you may take a step further to take these steps geared towards determining the overall effectiveness of your ads:

- **Don't lose track of your campaign goal**: This point has been hammered on already. Setting a campaign goal is important not only in achieving success, but also in determining what metrics are pertinent in measuring the impacts of your advertising effort.

- **Define success**: This is often missed while measuring the impacts of ads. For instance, if you set up a video ad to explain your product and then offer a link to your website where people can purchase that product, your ultimate goal would be to make sales.

If your video ends up getting a million views and very few or no sales at all, then it wouldn't be right to say that ad was successful. If however, the video ad was set up with the sole objective of garnering views, then a million views to its name would spell a tremendous success rate for the ad. It's important to draw out the goal of your advertising and define what success would mean to you in that campaign.

- **Know what metrics to utilize**: Metrics are the tools used in measuring the wellbeing of Facebook ads. The choice of metrics to use is tied to the chosen objective for a particular ad. For example, a mix of CPM, frequency, CTR and cost-per-click are the recommended metrics for the success of a lead generation ad, while a combination of impressions, CPM, frequency, amount spent, CTR, link clicks, CPC, leads, cost-per-lead should be chosen for awareness ads.

- **Create a report on your observation**: After choosing the appropriate metrics, the next step you should take is to monitor them on Ads Manager. You can then create a report on measurement, or feed the data compiled from the measuring process into a third-party analytics application or website to obtain a clear report.

Measuring the impacts of ads created to run on Facebook is a way of making certain that money is not thrown into thin air and allowed to disappear. It's a system of accountability which ensures that every cent spent is directed towards the overall success of your brand.

Leveraging the Facebook pixel

First off, we need to define what a pixel is. A pixel is a code that is placed on a website to track users' activities. Facebook pixel is designed to analyze activities on a host website, and allows marketers to measure the effectiveness of their advertising campaigns. While installed, Pixel can be used to monitor activities such as page visits, product views, and product purchases. This information is then sent to Facebook where it can be used for remarketing and retargeting purposes.

There are a myriad of ways you can use data collected from the Facebook pixel tool to improve your Facebook advertising strategy. We have listed some here.

- **Drive sales:** This is an obvious one. Facebook pixel tracking data can be used to set up automatic bidding to target people who are more likely to take required actions, such as making a purchase.

- **Track conversions:** Pixel makes it possible to track users' interaction with your website after seeing your ad. Tracking can be taken further to the type of devices people use in interacting with your website, whether it's a desktop or mobile.
- **Reaching the right people:** Facebook pixel allows you to find new customers, or people who have interacted with your website, and create lookalike audiences to reach more people who are like your best performing customers.
- **Measuring results:** Through the use of Facebook pixel, you can examine how successful your ads are by measuring the direct results, such as conversions and sales.

Setting up Facebook pixel on your website.

If you want to set up Facebook pixel on your website to track events (such as purchases and products views), Then follow these steps carefully.

1. First, you need to generate the pixel code. To do this, go to Ads Manager on the Facebook platform. Make your way to the navigation menu, and click on "Pixels" (under "Measure and Report").
2. Click "Set Up Pixel".
3. Click "Manually Install the Code Yourself".
4. Click "Continue".
5. Click "Install Events".

6. Select the event you'd like to track by clicking the toggle icon next to it.
7. Select "Track Event on Page Load" or "Track Event on Inline Action".
   - **Track Event on Page Load**: Choose this option if the action you care about can be tracked when someone lands on a certain page, like a confirmation page after completing a purchase.
   - **Track Event on Inline Action**: Choose this option if the action you want to track requires someone to click something (like an "add to cart" or "purchase" button).
8. Add event parameters, like Conversion Value or Currency, to measure additional information about your event (Recommended).

9. Copy this event code and paste it on the relevant page of your site. Be sure not to modify the pixel code you've already placed in the header of your website.

- For page load events: place the code just below the closing header section of the page (for many websites, this will be right after the opening <body> tag).
- For inline action events: add the event code between script tags next to the action you want to track (like a button).

This is the complete process of tracking an event on your website. If you would like to track more than one event, repeat these steps for the events you'd like to track. To err on the side of caution, make sure you have the Pixel Helper tool installed. Facebook Pixel Helper is a Chrome browser plugin (found in the Chrome web store) that helps you find out if your pixel is working adequately.

Benefits of using Facebook analytics

Facebook Analytics is a comprehensive tool that allows you to visualize your entire sales funnel, gauge and understand the lifetime value of users, and see how your organic posts and paid ads interrelate.

Better still, it's a free tool that requires only your Facebook page and pixel, and thrives within your Facebook ad account. Facebook Analytics assists you in understanding how people use your websites and apps.

With well over 2 billion monthly users and growing, Facebook analytics was built using the same tools, techniques, and infrastructure to help you grow your business. Whether your ads are focused on retention, engagement, or conversion, Analytics has the tools you need, including funnels, cohorts, segmentation, breakdown tables, automated push campaigns, and more.

It also provides in-depth demographic information and audience insights to help you better understand your audience, and more accurately analyze their behaviors.

Although the Facebook analytics tool is often used by advanced marketers, it's still an important tool that can be used by all brands, big and small. Below are essential benefits of using the analytics tool:

- **Visualizing your sales funnel**: Tracking a customer who liked your page days ago, then viewed some items on your website thereafter and finally made a purchase today used to be difficult, if not impossible. These complex data sets which were hitherto difficult to access, are now relatively easy to pin down with Facebook analytics.

- **Optimize your content**: With the information obtained from Facebook Analytics, you can understand which content is shared the most, and what days and times record the most engagements. This allows you to optimize to get the most out of your content.

In advertising, information is vital. And when that information is about the people who are very likely to make purchases and improve the financial status of a business, then it's invaluable. The Facebook Analytics tool is all about information – user demographics, page likes, video views, purchases, and so much more. A Facebook marketer can leverage on this world of data to lay out and implement impressive strategies to optimize ad content and drive success.

CHAPTER 5: CONCLUSIONS

Dos and don'ts of Facebook advertising

In this book, you've learned the best practices in creating and maintaining a successful Facebook marketing campaign.

From knowing how to set your advertising objective, to learning to write the best ad copies and lay out an interesting visual, you're definitely on your way to kick starting a massively engaging ad campaign.

But this learning process would be incomplete without a word of caution. Laid out in the next lines are some dos and don'ts of Facebook advertising that are sure to keep your ads free from errors when planning your next marketing campaign.

Dos

- **Split-test your ads**: Split testing (or A/B testing) allows you to test two different versions of an ad, so as to see what works and what doesn't, making it possible for you to improve future campaigns. While doing a split test, make sure that the two test ads are identical but for a single variable, so that you'll know why one of the ads outperformed the other.
- **Narrow down your audience**: Targeting is probably the most important step in the Facebook advertising process. Be sure not to make your targeting too broad, else you risk

spending too much money to get very little result. By narrowing down your audience, you create ads that appeal to that specific demographic.

- **Include a clear call-to-action**: Understand that Facebook users are not on the platform to see ads. That's why it's important to make your ads as direct and clear as possible. If you want your audience to take a specific action such as downloading an eBook or signing for newsletters, be sure to state it clearly and directly in your ad visual.

- **Use engaging visuals**: It's a fact that photos and videos speak louder than words, and are more likely to bring you success. Facebook users scroll though their news feed in a manner that makes write ups difficult to grab attention. High quality photos and videos however – when used effectively – does the trick.

Don'ts

- **Being dormant**: It's sad to see some advertisers do this. Facebook audiences are not bots or aliens, they're humans like you, so treat them as such.

  If the only time your fans see your post is when you're asking them to purchase a product or download your latest app, then they're apt to grow tired of your post and totally ignore you after that. Occasional *hellos* and quality posts (without any demands whatsoever) keeps your fans entertained and in sync with your page.

- **Making your ad copy too long**: Nobody likes too much text. Your audience aren't any different. Writing essay-long copies only gets viewers bored and tired. Instead, replace that extra text with an image that relates with your ad.

- **Being too loud**: Posting frequently on Facebook clutters your audience news feed and turns them off. If you do this, you risk being *unliked* by your existing fans. To support this assertion, a study conducted on the subject matter showed that about 70% of social media users unlike a brand's page on Facebook because the brand is posting too often.

When it comes down to ensuring the success of your brand in the Facebook marketing arena, the rules stated above are important to note. However, it's also pertinent to understand that all guidelines can't work for all campaigns, so pick what works for you and implement it religiously.

The Offer
Michael offered a 248-page hardcover book to any customer who bought at least $300 worth of bookbinding supplies

The Promotion
To kickstart the campaign, Michael sent out an email to let his 1,180 email contacts know about the social campaign

After all, he was offering a pretty great deal

He also started showing off all of the products that BookBinders Workshop had to offer by posting photos, comments, and news about upcoming events.

The Results
In one month, Michael's social campaign earned Bookbinders Workshop $15,000 in one month. The Page received 600 fans in one month, up from 50.

Case studies A: successful ads

We've compiled a few successful ads for you to chew on, including "the catch", that is, the ads' world changing ingredient. Make sure to analyze them further to find out why they were as successful as they were.

Case study I:

Goals achieved:

- An increase in fans from 50 to 650 in just a month.
- Increase in sales of $15,000.

The catch: An offer of a free 248-page hardcover book to anyone that bought $300 of book binding supplies.

Case study II:

The Offer
Elaine decided to give a 10% discount to anyone who liked the Page by placing a special code on the reveal Page of her campaign.

The Promotion
Elaine initially promoted her campaign by sending an email to her 1,767 email contacts.

She also posted photos of different products and a behind-the-scene look at the store to keep fans engaged.

The Results
In just 48 hours, Elaine says she saw $10,000 in profit from her social campaign.

Not only that, the Facebook Page's "likes" grew by 200% in three weeks.

Goals achieved:

- It produced a $10,000 profit
- Facebook page "likes" grew by 200% in just 3 weeks

The catch: The advertiser offered a 10% discount via a special code on a reveal page that clients saw after "liking" the Facebook page.

Case study III:

The Offer

Seconds & Surplus is a wholesale store where many sales are over $1,000.

Jay offered a coupon for 10% off, which meant that customers could save quite a bit of money.

The Promotion

Jay sent an email to 7,946 email subscribers showcasing the new Facebook offer.

He also started to regularly host Facebook surveys and quizzes, in addition to posting photos.

The Results

Jay launched the campaign on a Friday and, by Sunday, the discount generated $7,000. After one week, Jay says $12,000 in sales came directly from Facebook.

In one month, the campaign netted Seconds & Surplus $32,625.

A total of 37 coupons were redeemed and the fan count for the Seconds & Surplus Facebook Page tripled, from 150 to 450.

Goals achieved:

- $12,000 in sales directly from Facebook with total sales increase of over $32,000 in one month

- Increase in the Facebook fan count by 300%.

The catch: The marketer offered a coupon that gave a 10% discount after a Fan "liked" the page. Along with that he ran surveys, quizzes and posted photos to increase engagement.

Case study IV:

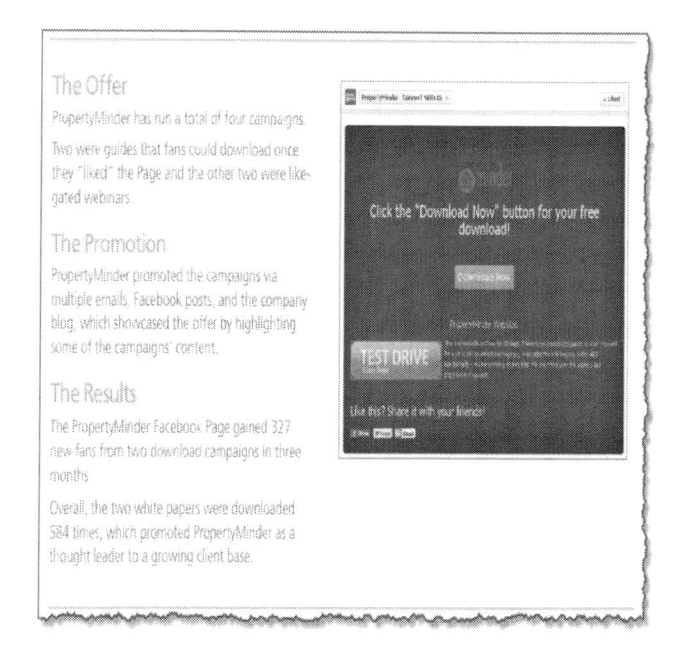

> **The Offer**
>
> PropertyMinder has run a total of four campaigns.
>
> Two were guides that fans could download once they "liked" the Page and the other two were like-gated webinars.
>
> **The Promotion**
>
> PropertyMinder promoted the campaigns via multiple emails, Facebook posts, and the company blog, which showcased the offer by highlighting some of the campaigns' content.
>
> **The Results**
>
> The PropertyMinder Facebook Page gained 327 new fans from two download campaigns in three months.
>
> Overall, the two white papers were downloaded 584 times, which promoted PropertyMinder as a thought leader to a growing client base.

Goals achieved:

- 327 new fans.
- 584 downloads of the whitepaper.

The catch: The advertiser offered a "Free Download" of a white paper.

Case studies B: Dead ads

Below are examples of ads that performed poorly on Facebook, including "the fall", that is, what they got wrong. Instead of showing pity for the advertisers that lost money on these ads, try to learn from their mistakes and improve your Facebook marketing strategy.

Case study I:

The fall: No clear call-to-action.

Case study II:

The fall: Too long ad copy.

Case study III:

> **Victoria's Property Secrets** added 25 new photos.
> Real Estate Service · 356 Likes · Yesterday at 6:35am
>
> Plumstead - 2 Bedroom Apartment For Sale - R950 000. To view contact Victoria on 078 044 4842
>
> Secure, open-plan apartment with gorgeous views in all directions!
>
> This delightful, spacious, east-facing apartment gets sunshine all day long and has a balcony for enjoying those spectacular views. You can see all the way to the Helderberg Mountains on a clear day! The apartment has 2 large bedrooms, large open-plan lounge, dining area and kitchen, separate toilet and a bathroom... See More

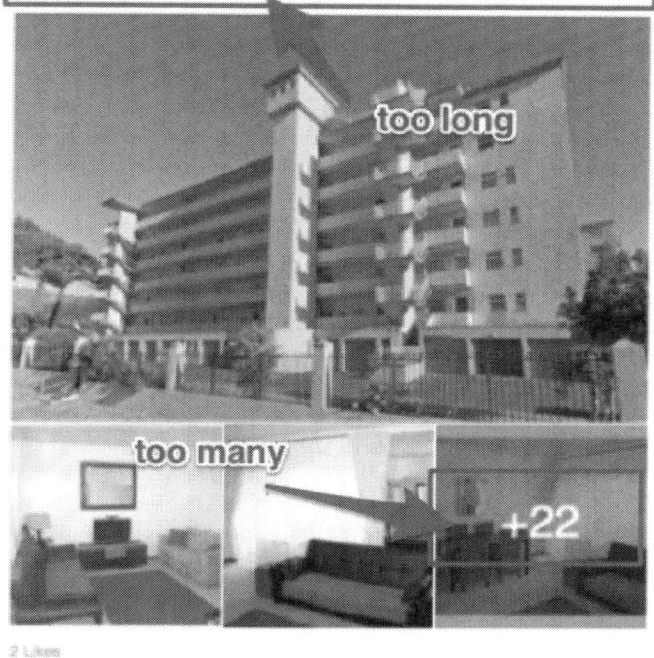

too long

too many

+22

2 Likes

The fall: Too much text and too many visuals.

Case study IV:

The fall: Inadequate ad copy.

WRAP UP

Facebook advertising, to some, is as simple as pushing a bit of text mixed with a slice of visual out into the open. You know better. Marketing on Facebook – or any other digital marketing platform – is an art that can only be perfected through the mastering of certain prerequisite skills.

What this book has done is highlighting these all-important skills and offering guidelines that are guaranteed to land you some, if not all, of them to take your advertising venture to the skies.

While it's easy for your advertising campaigns to drown in the pool of advertising schemes created by over 2 million marketers worldwide, the ideas in this book have been tested to make your ad campaigns stand out, stand firm, and most importantly, bring currency into your pockets.

Printed in Great Britain
by Amazon